# WONDERS OF THE

# NATURAL WORLD

# WONDERS OF THE NATURAL WORLD

Written by **David Burnie**

# DK

## LONDON, NEW YORK, MELBOURNE, MUNICH, AND DELHI

**Illustration spreads written by** Andrea Mills

**Senior editor** Andrea Mills

**Art editor** Marilou Prokopiou

**Senior art editor** Smiljka Surla

**Managing editor** Linda Esposito

**Managing art editor** Diane Thistlethwaite

**Publishing manager** Andrew Macintyre

**Category publisher** Laura Buller

**Design development manager**
Sophia M. Tampakopoulos

**Picture researcher** Fran Vargo

**Production controller** Erica Rosen

**DTP designer** Siu Chan, Andy Hilliard

**Jacket editor** Mariza O'Keeffe

**Jacket designer** Smiljka Surla

**Consultant** Kim Dennis-Bryan

**Illustrations** László Veres

Published in the United States in 2007 by
DK Publishing
375 Hudson Street
New York, NY 10014

Copyright © 2007 Dorling Kindersley Limited
07 08 09 10 11 10 9 8 7 6 5 4 3 2 1
GD066 – 07/07

ISBN: 978-0-75662-980-9

Jacket color reproduction by Colourscan, Singapore
Inside color reproduction by GRB Editrice, UK
Printed and bound in China by Hung Hing

**Discover more at
www.dk.com**

# Contents

# Wonders of the world

This is the start of a journey to the most spectacular places on Earth. From mountain peaks to desert dunes, erupting volcanoes to calm coral reefs, and deep canyons to tropical rain forests, this route around the world encompasses every continent and includes the most amazing scenery and extraordinary wildlife on the planet.

**Norwegian Fjords**

**NORTH AMERICA**

**Grand Canyon**

**ATLANTIC OCEAN**

**Grand Canyon**
Carved by the Colorado River, the Grand Canyon is made of rocks up to 2 billion years old. With dizzying cliffs and towering pinnacles, the canyon offers stunning views at sunset.

**Mauna Loa**

**PACIFIC OCEAN**

**Mauna Loa**
The world's biggest volcano—Mauna Loa—rose through the surface of the Pacific Ocean almost half a million years ago. Its massive slopes contain enough lava and ash to bury New York State in a layer 1,650 ft (500 m) deep.

**Amazon Rain forest**

**Norwegian Fjords**
Ice started to gouge out deep valleys on Norway's western coast thousands of years ago. Today, most of the ice has gone, and the valleys have turned into fjords. With their steep sides and still water, the fjords are one of Europe's most popular vacation destinations.

**SOUTH AMERICA**

**Antarctica**
Smothered by its vast ice cap, Antarctica is by far the coldest continent on Earth. But despite the harsh climate, the sea surrounding this frozen continent has a variety of wildlife, including penguins and whales.

**Antarctica**

**Amazon Rain forest**
The Amazon Rain forest has more species of plants and animals living side by side than anywhere else in the world. However, this natural wonder is fast disappearing, as the forest's giant trees are felled.

ASIA

EUROPE

FRICA

AUSTRALIA

PACIFIC OCEAN

**Mount Everest**
First climbed in 1953, Mount Everest is the tallest mountain on Earth. With its high winds, blizzards, and ice falls, the summit is notoriously dangerous, but its lower slopes are home to some fascinating animals and plants.

**Great Barrier Reef**
Thousands of years in the making, Australia's Great Barrier Reef is the greatest underwater wonder in the world. Brightly colored corals create a home for a wide variety of fish in these clear, warm waters.

Mount Everest

Rift Valley

Namib Desert

Great Barrier Reef

**Rift Valley**
Valleys don't come any bigger than the Rift—an enormous trench that slices its way through East Africa, and then onward into the Middle East. The Rift is famous for its wildlife, which includes the largest herds of grazing mammals in the world.

**Namib Desert**
With its huge sand dunes and mist-shrouded coast, the Namib is a unique desert. Far from being empty, it is home to some bizarre animals and plants, which have successfully adapted to a land where there is a lot of fog, but very little rain.

Deep enough to swallow the world's tallest building with plenty of room to spare, the Grand Canyon is one of the most breathtaking sights on Earth. It measures 1 mile (1.7 km) in height and more than 280 miles (450 km) in length, with cliffs and peaks that started forming almost two billion years ago. The vast chasm was created by the Colorado River, which has slowly gouged its way through this high mountain plain.

# Grand Canyon

## High and dry

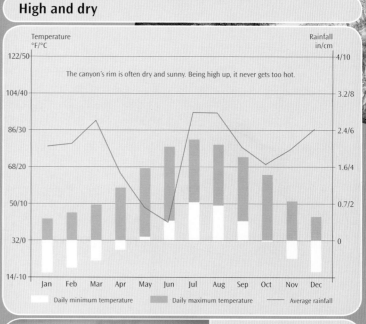

The canyon's rim is often dry and sunny. Being high up, it never gets too hot.

| | Temperature °F/°C | | Rainfall in/cm |

Daily minimum temperature · Daily maximum temperature · Average rainfall

### Climate of choice

The canyon is so deep that there is often a big temperature difference between the top and the bottom. In winter, the canyon's rim can be covered with snow, but it can be as warm as a summer's day down by the river.

**Satellite view**
The Grand Canyon slices through the Colorado Plateau—a huge plain, west of the Rocky Mountains. The plain is dry and dusty for most of the year, but it is home to hardy trees and shrubs, as well as a variety of wildlife.

**Ancient cliffs**
The canyon's cliffs are made of sedimentary rock, with the oldest rocks near the bottom, and the most recent ones at the top. River water has eaten away at the rock by scraping it with sand and grit.

**High falls**
Some of the smaller streams flowing into the Colorado River form waterfalls. One of the most beautiful is the Havasu Falls, where crystal-clear water plunges more than 100 ft (30 m) into a shady creek.

**Colorado River**
From its source in the Rocky Mountains to its exit in the Pacific Ocean, the Colorado River covers 1,430 miles (2,300 km). In the past, the river was left wild, but now it is controlled by some of the world's tallest dams.

**Spectacular sunset**
The most dramatic time to see the Grand Canyon is in the evening, when the sinking sun appears to set the rocks on fire. As the sun drops, the rock layers light up, revealing oranges, coppers, and golds. Finally, only the highest pinnacles catch the light, before the entire canyon disappears into darkness.

**Rafting the river**
Millions of people visit the Grand Canyon every year. The most adventurous travel down the Colorado River on inflatable rafts. This is a difficult journey, which includes choppy white water and takes several days to complete.

# North face

The remote North Rim of the Grand Canyon lies in northern Arizona. Here, the giant gorge has steep walls, with panoramic views to the south, east, and west. Due to its elevation 8,000 ft (2,400 m) above sea level, the North Rim has the coolest temperatures and the cleanest air. The canyon's creatures live in this area, from the rocky top, to the fast-flowing river.

**◀ California condor**
A weighty bird, the condor can fly 150 miles (250 km) in a single day, and live for more than 50 years.

**◀ Bighorn sheep**
Herds of these nimble sheep climb around the cliffs. Group leaders are determined by horn size.

**◀ Wild burros**
Originally from Africa, hardy burros feed on local grasses and stay close to the river for water.

**Fremont cottonwood ▶**
The flowery cottonwood grows very rapidly on low, moist ground.

**Coyote ▼**
Part of the dog family, this solitary stalker hunts small mammals, such as beavers.

**▼ American beaver**
Aquatic plants are food for this beaver, who can stay submerged in the river for 15 minutes.

**◀ Gunnison's prairie dogs**
These plump rodents guard their burrow entrances and sound a loud call to warn of predators.

**◀ Cholla cactus**
Hot, rocky ground suits the cholla cactus, with its flowers blooming from April until June.

**American dippers ▶**
A special, extra set of eyelids gives these songbirds good underwater vision, as they fish in the river.

**Blackbrush ▶**
Seen all over the canyon, this low-growing, evergreen shrub flowers in summer.

**Giant hairy scorpions ▶**
These scorpions are pincer to pincer as they perform a courtship "dance" before mating.

**Violet green swallow ▶**
Usually seen in flight, this colorful bird builds its nest in crevices near water.

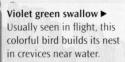

**Cougar ▶**
A lone hunter, this fast-moving cat chases large prey, such as bighorn sheep.

**Utah juniper ▲**
With its multiforked trunk and plentiful roots, this tree gets maximum moisture.

**▼ Peregrine falcon**
At speeds of 200 mph (320 kph), this high-flying falcon swoops from the sky to attack its prey.

**Bald eagle ▶**
The national bird of the US, the bald eagle can fly at speeds of 40 mph (65 kph).

**Utah agave ▶**
The flowering, fruit-bearing agave grows very quickly, to heights of 15 ft (4 m).

**▼ Great blue heron**
The US's largest heron has a croaky call and is most often seen wading and fishing in the river.

**◀ Barrel cactus**
Named after its barrel shape, this cactus can grow to 10 ft (3 m), and bears spines and flowers.

**Rattlesnake ▼**
Known for the warning rattle in its tail, the rattlesnake has sharp fangs and a venomous bite.

**Rock squirrel ▶**
The canyon cliffs are an ideal location for this secretive squirrel to build its den.

**Long-tailed pocket mice ▶**
Cheek pouches help these mice to store food temporarily, while larger supplies are kept in their burrows.

**◀ Gila monster**
This poisonous lizard releases venom from a gland in its jaw when biting into prey.

**◀ Mountain short-horned lizard**
Beetles, grasshoppers, ants, and small snakes may all find themselves on this lizard's tongue.

# Grand tour

Stunning views are just one part of the Grand Canyon story. Far below the canyon's rim is a hidden haven of wildlife. Birds and butterflies use the canyon as a private highway, while barrel-shaped cacti cling to the huge cliffs. All of this exists because the Colorado River has carved its way downward through thousands of yards of rock. The river is still hard at work today.

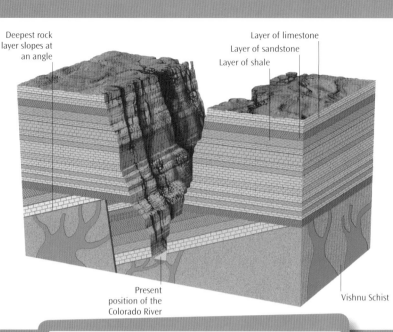

Deepest rock layer slopes at an angle

Layer of limestone
Layer of sandstone
Layer of shale

Present position of the Colorado River

Vishnu Schist

### How the canyon formed
The Grand Canyon began forming about 5 million years ago, when the Colorado River began cutting its way through deep layers of crumbling rock. At the bottom of the canyon is a dark, hard rock called the Vishnu Schist. This rock is about 2 billion years old.

Flowers open in early spring

Base of flower swells up into a prickly fruit

Middle of the stem holds sap

Cactus swells as it soaks up water

Rows of sharp spines

Roots spread out to collect water

### Migrating monarchs
In spring and fall, monarch butterflies often travel through the canyon on their annual migration. These butterflies fly north to Canada to breed, but they spend the winter in warmer places, such as the coast of California, and the mountains of northern Mexico. At the height of the migration, millions of butterflies are on the move.

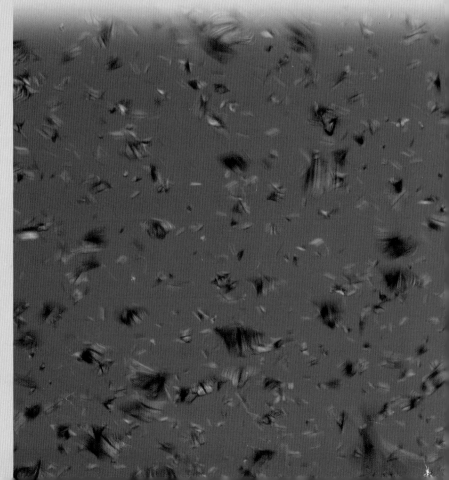

### Core of the cactus
Cacti are experts at surviving the summer heat, because they store water in their stems. They soak water up through their wide roots and store it in their juicy green flesh. The spines deter thirsty animals from helping themselves to this private water supply. Cacti also have colorful flowers, which attract insects and birds.

Acorn jammed
tightly into hole

Tough beak used for
chiseling holes in bark

New acorn ready to
be pushed into place

Same tree is used
year after year

Strong claws for
gripping bark

Males and
females have
bright red heads

## Acorn woodpeckers

These busy birds live
in the pine trees on the
canyon's south rim. They
peck holes in trees, then
collect acorns and store them
individually inside. A single
"granary tree" can contain
50,000 acorns—enough to keep
its owners well-fed through winter.
If other woodpeckers come near,
the owners chase them away.

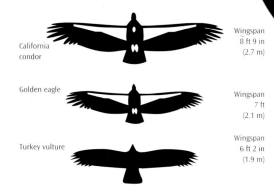

California
condor

Wingspan
8 ft 9 in
(2.7 m)

Golden eagle

Wingspan
7 ft
(2.1 m)

Turkey vulture

Wingspan
6 ft 2 in
(1.9 m)

## Return of the condor

The California condor is North America's biggest
flying bird. In the 1980s, this huge vulture almost
became extinct, when only 22 birds were left.
Since then, condors have been bred in captivity
and released into the wild. There are now more
than 130 wild condors, and about 170 others in
breeding stations and zoos.

## A frozen world

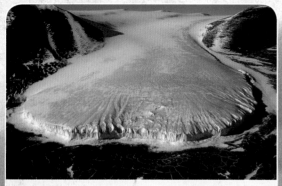

**Moving ice**
More than 97 percent of Antarctica is covered by ice. From the center of the continent, this ice is constantly on the move, feeding ice streams and giant glaciers, which slowly creep toward the sea.

**Barren land**
The Dry Valleys are one of the few ice-free places on the continent, with no snow falling for more than a million years. This area is so desolate that landers destined for Mars have been tested here.

**Ice shelves**
Vast ice shelves often form where glaciers meet the coast. The Ross Ice Shelf is the biggest, with an area about the size of France. At the edges, the shelves crack and separate, creating icebergs, which drift out to sea.

**Offshore islands**
The ocean around Antarctica is dotted with islands, such as Kerguelen, Bouvet, and South Georgia. Despite being lashed by ferocious winds, these tiny specks of land are breeding grounds for millions of seals and birds.

**The big freeze**
A record low temperature of -126°F (-89°C) was recorded at the Russian Antarctic base of Vostok in 1983. As well as being the coldest continent, Antarctica is also the highest and driest. Most of the continent gets less than 2 in (5 cm) of snow a year, which makes it drier than the Sahara Desert.

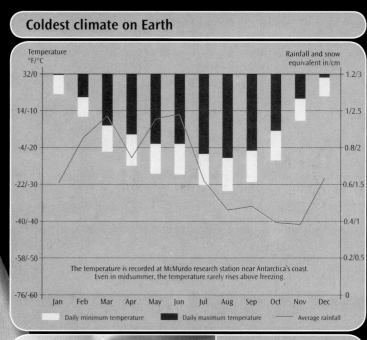

South Orkney
Islands

Scotia Sea

Antarctic Circle

South
Shetland
Islands

Dronning Maud
Land

Weddell Sea

Larsen
Ice Shelf

Coats
Land

Antarctic Peninsula

Berkner
Island

Filchner
Ice Shelf

Alexander
Island

Ronne Ice
Shelf

ANTARCTICA

Bellingshausen
Sea

Ellsworth
Land

South
Pole

In January 1820, the Russian explorer Captain Fabian von Bellingshausen became the first person to set eyes on Antarctica—the coldest continent on Earth. Antarctica is covered by a huge ice sheet up to 3 miles (4.7 km) thick, and in winter, the temperature drops so low that skin freezes in seconds. As a result, it is the least explored place on the planet, but amazingly, wildlife thrives here.

# Antarctica

### Coldest climate on Earth

Temperature
°F/°C

Rainfall and snow
equivalent in/cm

| | | | | | | | | | | | |
|---|---|---|---|---|---|---|---|---|---|---|---|
| 32/0 | | | | | | | | | | | 1.2/3 |
| 14/-10 | | | | | | | | | | | 1/2.5 |
| -4/-20 | | | | | | | | | | | 0.8/2 |
| -22/-30 | | | | | | | | | | | 0.6/1.5 |
| -40/-40 | | | | | | | | | | | 0.4/1 |
| -58/-50 | | | | | | | | | | | 0.2/0.5 |
| -76/-60 | | | | | | | | | | | 0 |
| Jan | Feb | Mar | Apr | May | Jun | Jul | Aug | Sep | Oct | Nov | Dec |

The temperature is recorded at McMurdo research station near Antarctica's coast. Even in midsummer, the temperature rarely rises above freezing.

 Daily minimum temperature ▮ Daily maximum temperature — Average rainfall

**Gale-force winds**
Antarctica is also the windiest continent. Freezing air pours downhill from the central ice cap, sometimes gusting at more than 185 mph (300 kph) where it meets the coast. These gales can last for days at a time.

**Scientific research**
Antarctica's human population consists almost entirely of scientists. Research stations have been set up, which the scientists use as a base. They carry out many different kinds of area analysis, from cosmology to oceanography. Here a scientist is exploring the underside of an ice shelf, in water that is close to freezing.

# Ice stage

A landscape of mountains, glaciers, and ice floes makes the Antarctic Peninsula one of the world's last great wildernesses. This peninsula enjoys the mildest climate of the whole continent, so the area is a wonderland for wildlife. Gulls swoop low over the icy waters of the Weddell Sea, as penguins plunge in to find fish and whales splash about during their feeding frenzy.

**▼ Adelie penguins**
In their quest to find fish, these deep-sea divers can reach 550 ft (170 m) under water.

**Killer whale ▶**
Top of the food chain, this whale has no predators and eats 550 lb (250 kg) of food a day.

**▲ Snow petrel**
Never upset a snow petrel. Their defense mechanism is to squirt waxy stomach oil!

**Emperor penguin ▶**
The largest of all the penguins, the emperor is a very strong swimmer.

**▲ Kelp gull**
This scavenger of the sea eats anything, including fish, crabs, and other birds.

**South polar skua ▶**
The powerful skua battles other seabirds for food, even killing them if necessary.

**Cape petrel ▶**
Due to its patterned wings and back, the cape petrel is nicknamed "the painted one."

**Antarctic tern ▶**
Large flocks of hundreds of sociable terns live, fish, and fly together.

**▼ Wilson's storm petrel**
This bird feeds by running along the surface of the sea with its beak submerged.

Dronning Maud Land

Coats Land

South Pole

A N T A R C T I C A

Weddell Sea

Ellsworth Land

South Orkney Islands

South Shetland Islands

Antarctic Peninsula

Larsen Ice Shelf

Ronne Ice Shelf

Berkner Island

Filchner Ice Shelf

Bellingshausen Sea

60°S

70°S

Antarctic Circle

**Crabeater seals ▼**
These seals eat krill (tiny marine life), not crabs. Their "strainer" teeth keep the krill but expel water.

**Weddell seal ▲**
Staying under water for up to an hour, this seal uses its strong teeth to bite a breathing hole in the ice.

**▲ Bubble-net feeding**
Humpbacks group under water and swim up, blowing bubbles. These trap small prey for the whales to eat.

**▼ Snowy sheathbill**
The only bird in Antarctica without webbed feet, the fluffy sheathbill looks for food on land.

**▼ Bald notothen**
The scales of the bald notothen include an antifreeze substance, which protects it against the cold.

**Lichen ▲**
Composed of aquatic algae and fungi, slow-growing lichen is found in very cold environments.

**▼ Humpback whales**
Acrobatic humpbacks can breach (jump) from the water. They travel in pods singing long "songs."

**▲ Chinstrap penguins**
Nicknamed "stone-crackers" due to their harsh call, chinstraps are really named after the black chin feathers.

**◄ Kelp**
Tiny marine creatures, which some seabirds eat, hide in this thick seaweed.

# Life on the ice

Antarctica has not always been cold. Millions of years ago it lay much farther north and was home to plants and even dinosaurs. But as it moved southward, the climate got colder, and the entire continent was gradually covered in ice. Today, many animals live in the sea around Antarctica, but very few breed on the ice itself. The most spectacular exception are emperor penguins. Female emperors lay a single egg in the fall, leaving the males to take charge of the eggs. The males incubate the eggs through winter, in the freezing darkness of the polar night.

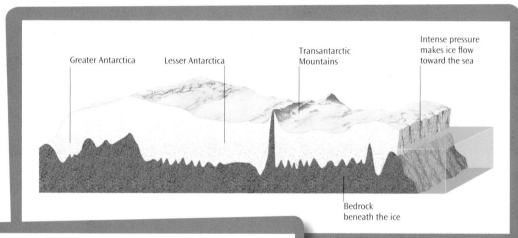

Greater Antarctica

Lesser Antarctica

Transantarctic Mountains

Intense pressure makes ice flow toward the sea

Bedrock beneath the ice

**Under the ice cap**
Antarctica's ice cap is shaped like a giant dome, split into two parts by the Transantarctic Mountains. Ice has built up from falling snow and the deepest layers are millions of years old. The ice creeps toward the sea in huge glaciers—some are more than 60 miles (100 km) wide.

Back legs are used for swimming

Front legs are used to collect floating food

**Krill**
These shrimplike creatures live in the Southern Ocean. They are only about 2 in (6 cm) in length, but they form huge swarms that can weigh millions of tons. Krill are a vital food for many Antarctic animals. Penguins catch them one by one, but whales scoop them up by the mouthful as they plough through the slow-moving swarms.

**Ice packs**
In blizzard conditions, adult emperors huddle together in large groups to keep themselves warm. The birds on the outside constantly push their way in toward the center so that they all take turns at being protected from the icy wind.

## Seabed seasons

**Winter warmer**
Emperor penguins don't build nests. Instead, the female passes her egg to the male, who keeps it warm by putting it on his feet. He then covers the egg with a flap of feathery skin, keeping it snug. The egg's temperature stays at 107°F (42°C) all through the winter, even when it is -76°F (-60°C) outside.

**Summer**
Despite the near-freezing temperatures, the Antarctic seabed teems with life. Many animals live near the edge of the ice. They include fish, sea anemones, sea urchins, starfish, and some soft types of coral.

**Winter**
When summer comes to an end, the sea freezes over, and the ice shelves spread farther out. Animals in the shallows move to deeper water to keep from being crushed to pieces by the ice.

**Squirrel monkey** ► During the day, this monkey races around the trees, using its tail to balance.

▼ **Coati** This furry member of the raccoon family enjoys a diet of insects.

**Leaf hoppers** ► These insects have piercing mouthparts so they can suck the sap of plants.

► **Green iguana** The tree-dwelling, leaf-eating green iguana is an agile climber and a fast runner.

► **Anolis lizard** If this lizard's huge throat flashes red, he is threatening males or attracting females.

**Ceiba tree** The ceiba needs lots of water and sunlight. The Amazon's heavy rain and hot weather are ideal.

▼ **Amazon poison frog** Poison frogs are brightly colored to warn predators that their skin secretes harmful toxins.

**Termite nest** ► Tree termites make nests using chewed-up wood and soil, mixed with their droppings.

**Scarlet macaw** ► This large, noisy parrot can fly at 35 mph (56 kph) and live for 80 years.

► **Leaf-cutter ants** Lines of ants carrying leaves have been seen stretching over 800 ft (250 m)!

**Red-bellied macaw** ► Named after the tiny red patch on its belly, this green bird has a high-pitched scream!

# Tall tree

The ceiba tree is one of the tallest in the Amazon Rain Forest. Also known as the kapok, it can grow to 150 ft (45 m) in height and live for more than 500 years. The ceiba flourishes in seasonally flooded areas of the tropical rain forest, such as the Mamirauá Reserve. Its branches, leaves, and bark are home to many animals, birds, and insects, while rare flowers and thick vines grow up and down the trunk.

**Harpy eagle ▶**
With a wingspan of 7 ft (2 m), the harpy is one of the world's largest birds of prey.

**▼ Southern tamandua**
Part of the anteater family, the tamandua can climb trees using its strong claws.

**▼ Chestnut-fronted macaw**
The tail of this beaky bird makes up half its entire size of 18 in (45 cm).

**◀ Hoatzin**
A poor flier, the hoatzin spends most of its time in trees, eating the leaves.

**▲ Kinkajou**
This mammal hates sudden noise. If disturbed, it will scream, claw, and bite!

**▲ Emerald tree boa**
This meat-eating snake catches prey with its teeth, squeezes it to death, and swallows it whole.

**▲ Vampire bat**
This flying mammal hunts at night and spends every day asleep in the trees.

**Wasp nest ▶**
These nests usually hang near branches and leaves for extra protection.

**Tarantula ▶**
The world's biggest, hairiest spiders live in the Amazon Rain Forest.

**▼ Three-toed sloth**
The sloth is slow on land and prefers to be up a tree. It likes to eat and sleep upside down!

Covering more than one half of Brazil, the Amazon Rain Forest is the largest remaining tropical rain forest anywhere on Earth. Named after the Amazon River, which flows through the forest, the area is home to one-third of all the world's plant and animal species. Many birds, insects, and reptiles rely on the tall trees for food and shelter, as do the tribes of Amazonian Indians who have lived in the rain forest for thousands of years.

# Amazon Rain Forest

## Climate in the tropics

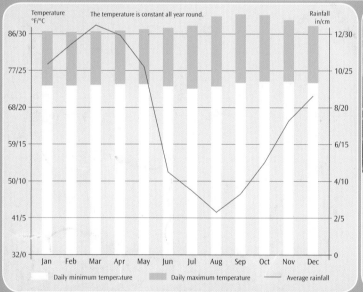

The temperature is constant all year round.

| Temperature °F/°C | | Rainfall in/cm |
|---|---|---|

Daily minimum temperature    Daily maximum temperature    Average rainfall

**Seasonal flooding**
Large sections of the rain forest are affected by flooding. In the rainy season, the Amazon River bursts its banks, covering the forest in up to 40 ft (12 m) of water. The flood can spread 12 miles (20 km) inland.

**Amazonian people**
At one time, more than five million native Indians lived here, but now only about 200,000 remain. Most tribes live as shifting cultivators, which means they settle to hunt and grow crops, then move on. This lets the soil recover its fertility. These tribesmen are performing a ceremonial dance.

**Record-breaking river**
The Amazon carries more water than any other river. It starts high in the snowcapped Andes in Peru, then flows 4,000 miles (6,435 km) across Peru and Brazil to its mouth in the Atlantic Ocean. In parts, the Amazon is so wide that you cannot see from one bank to the other.

### Mountain high
The Amazon River begins in the foothills of the Andes Mountains in Peru. It then flows across South America to the Atlantic Ocean. For more than half of its length, the Amazon flows through Brazil.

### Water features
Before it enters the enormous Amazon Basin, the Amazon River rushes down stunning waterfalls and through gorges. Other water features along the river's route include streams, lakes, torrents, and swamps.

### Canopy layer
The roof of the rain forest is the canopy. The leaves of these tall trees are dense, filtering out 80 percent of the sunlight. These leaves are pointed, so water drips off, and fungi cannot form.

### Deforestation
Over the years, huge areas of the forest have been cut down to provide timber, to make way for farmland, or to relocate people. If this rate of deforestation continues, there will be no forest left by the end of the century.

**Capybaras** ◄
The capybara is the largest living rodent. It loves to swim in the waters of the Amazon.

**Bromeliad** ►
Exclusive to the Americas, these flowering plants grow all around the rain forest.

**Anthurium** ▼
These flowers thrive in wet, tropical forest. New species are found every year.

**Scorpion** ►
This arachnid has a real sting in its tail—two venom sacs and an injecting barb lurk inside!

**Amazon kingfisher** ▼
This bird often perches on rocks or branches by water before diving in to catch fish.

**Giant otter** ◄
This otter lives in a family group under tree roots or fallen logs near the water's edge.

**Black caiman** ►
The caiman is a large carnivorous reptile that lives in slow-moving waters.

**Tapir** ►
Water is a must for tapirs. They enjoy swimming and walking along the riverbeds.

**Seasonal river flooding**
During periods of heavy rainfall, the river bursts its banks, flooding the forest.

**Pink dolphin** ►
This friendly mammal is very intelligent, with a brain capacity 40 percent bigger than ours.

**Manatee** ▼
Nicknamed "sea cow," the manatee spends its time grazing in shallow waters.

**Cichlids** ◄
Consisting of more than 1,000 different types, cichlids vary in size, shape, and color.

**Giant Amazon River turtle** ►
This big turtle weighs about 100 lb (45 kg) and measures more than 3 ft (1 m) in length.

**Piranhas** ▼
These carnivorous freshwater fish are known for their razor-sharp teeth and huge appetites.

**Arapaima** ►
Up to 8 ft (2.5 m) in length, this gigantic fish can leap out of the water to catch birds.

**▼ Fieldfare**
A brightly colored thrush, the fieldfare nests in trees and feeds insects and worms to its babies.

**Arctic fox ▲**
At high altitude, this fast, furry fox chases small prey, such as lemmings and birds.

**Brown bear ▶**
From grass and berries, to rodents and lemmings, this huge bear's diet depends on what is available.

**▲ Gyr falcon**
The largest in the falcon family, this bird can swoop on prey midair or on the ground.

**Stoats ▶**
Alert and agile, stoats are active day and night. Females protect their young and teach them to hunt.

**▼ Otter**
This skilled swimmer stays dry and warm because its soft fur is protected by a layer of waterproof hairs.

**Common porpoise ▲**
Though it is one of the smallest marine mammals, the porpoise eats up to 10 lb (4 kg) of small fish a day.

**◀ Oystercatcher**
The name suggests that this noisy, wading bird eats oysters, but it prefers worms and insects.

**▲ Atlantic wild salmon**
Young salmon eat tiny marine life, while adult salmon, which can weigh 70 lb (30 kg), eat large fish and eels.

**▼ Black-headed gulls**
With their loud, distinct call, the scientific name for these birds means "laughing gull"!

**▲ Common frog**
Cold, wet areas suit frogs. By breathing through its skin, this frog hibernates under water in winter.

# Focus on the fjords

Thousands of years ago Norway's coastline was covered in ice, and the climate stayed the same all year round. Now that the ice has melted and the fjords have formed, there are separate seasons and changing temperatures. Some animals come and go as food becomes available or scarce, while others, such as the red wood ant, make permanent homes. Their nests start off small, but years later, they can be 5 ft (1.5 m) tall, with more than a million residents.

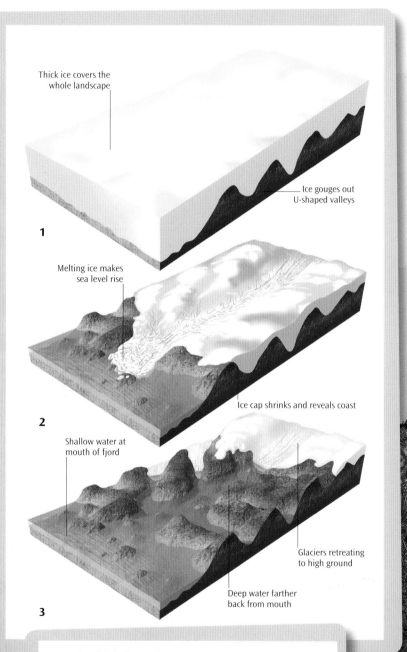

Thick ice covers the whole landscape

Ice gouges out U-shaped valleys

**1**

Melting ice makes sea level rise

Ice cap shrinks and reveals coast

**2**

Shallow water at mouth of fjord

Glaciers retreating to high ground

Deep water farther back from mouth

**3**

### How the fjords formed
**1** During the last Ice Age, Norway's present coastline was completely covered by an ice cap. The sea was much lower than it is today, and the ice gouged out deep valleys as it flowed downhill.
**2** When the climate warmed up, the ice cap started to melt, and the sea level began to rise. As the glaciers retreated, the sea flooded the valleys they had made.
**3** Today, most of the ice cap has melted, and the valleys have turned into fjords. At the mouth of each fjord, there is often a shallow underwater sill made from rocks that the glaciers dropped into the sea.

### Nest-building
Red wood ants make their nests out of fallen pine needles and twigs, heaping them into a mound. The surface of a nest works like a thatched roof, keeping the ants dry inside. During the summer, the ants are busy collecting food, but in the winter, they stay deep inside the nest.

### Nursery area
Each nest contains a complex network of tunnels and chambers. Some of the chambers are reserved for eggs, while others contain developing larvae. When a larva is fully grown, it seals itself in a silk cocoon. After several days, the cocoon splits open and an adult ant climbs out.

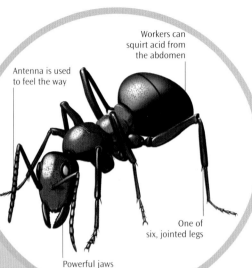

**Ant anatomy**
Wingless red wood ants have narrow waists and long antennae or feelers. Their eyes are small, and they find their way mainly by touch and smell. Worker ants have powerful jaws, which they use to collect nesting material and food.

Antenna is used to feel the way

Workers can squirt acid from the abdomen

One of six, jointed legs

Powerful jaws

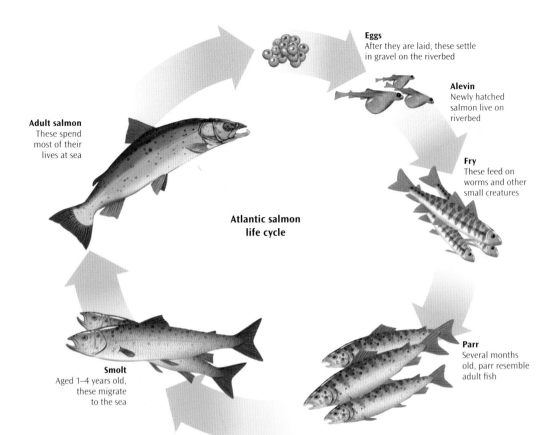

**Atlantic salmon life cycle**

**Eggs**
After they are laid, these settle in gravel on the riverbed

**Alevin**
Newly hatched salmon live on riverbed

**Fry**
These feed on worms and other small creatures

**Parr**
Several months old, parr resemble adult fish

**Smolt**
Aged 1–4 years old, these migrate to the sea

**Adult salmon**
These spend most of their lives at sea

## Return from the sea

Norway's coast is famous for its salmon, which migrate through the fjords on their way upstream to breed. Every river has a unique taste, so by tasting the water, adult salmon find their way back to the rivers where they were born. Female salmon lay their eggs on the riverbed. After the young have hatched, they go through several life stages before migrating back to sea.

## Seasonal coats

**Summer style**
The Arctic fox lives on the high ground above the fjords, where there are few places to hide. In summer, its fur is dark brown. This color provides camouflage, helping the fox to blend in with the rocks as it searches for food.

**Winter wardrobe**
In winter, most Arctic foxes grow white fur that camouflages them in the snow. This fur is long and thick, so it keeps the foxes warm as they hunt. In extremely cold conditions, foxes stay in their underground dens.

# Rift Valley

Millions of years ago, a gigantic trench formed in East Africa. It was created when heat deep under the ground slowly split the surface apart. This trench was 4,000 miles (6,400 km) in length and 60 miles (100 km) in width, with huge, sheer sides. As a result, it became known as the Great Rift Valley. Characterized by active volcanoes, hot springs, and deep lakes, this valley is best known for its vast expanses of grassland, where a wide range of wildlife lives.

SUDAN
ETHIOPIA
Great Rift Valley
UGANDA
KENYA
SOMALIA
DEMOCRATIC REPUBLIC OF THE CONGO
RWANDA
BURUNDI
Great Rift Valley
Great Rift Valley
INDIAN OCEAN
TANZANIA
ZAMBIA
MALAWI
MOZAMBIQUE

## Guide to the grasslands

### Water holes
In the Rift Valley, water holes are essential for survival. Some animals get the water they need from their food, but many mammals and birds need a daily drink. Predators know this and wait near water holes to catch their prey.

### Volcanoes
The Rift Valley was created by volcanic heat, and the valley floor is still studded with active volcanoes. Ol Doinyo Lengai, in Tanzania, is one of the biggest. It stands nearly 10,000 ft (3,000 m) in height and last erupted in 2006.

### Grazers
Much of the Rift Valley is grassland. This habitat provides food for many animals. The grass is eaten by wild mammals, including antelope, zebras, and buffalo, as well as cattle and goats belonging to local herdsmen.

### Kopjes
In many parts of East Africa, including the Rift Valley, there are piles of eroded rock, called kopjes. Lions use them as lookout posts, while small animals hide away in their crevices and cracks.

## Mass migration

Seen from the air, zebras and wildebeest migrate across the grassy plains of the Rift Valley's Masai Mara National Park, Kenya, in search of food and water. Together with the Serengeti National Park, in neighboring Tanzania, this wildlife reserve is home to the biggest herds of grazing mammals anywhere on Earth.

## A two-season climate

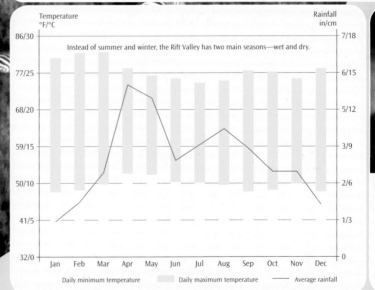

Instead of summer and winter, the Rift Valley has two main seasons—wet and dry.

| Temperature °F/°C | | Rainfall in/cm |
|---|---|---|
| 86/30 | | 7/18 |
| 77/25 | | 6/15 |
| 68/20 | | 5/12 |
| 59/15 | | 3/9 |
| 50/10 | | 2/6 |
| 41/5 | | 1/3 |
| 32/0 | Jan Feb Mar Apr May Jun Jul Aug Sep Oct Nov Dec | 0 |

Daily minimum temperature　　Daily maximum temperature　　—— Average rainfall

### Storm front

The wet season usually sta[rts] in March, when thunderclouds gather over the Rift Valley. Once the rain gets underway, the grass starts to sprout, and the entire landscape changes from dry brown to lush green.

### Masai tribe

The Masai are one of the largest tribes in the Rift Valley region. Traditionally, they live by herding cattle and goats. Instead of staying in one place, they keep on the move, traveling to wherever the grazing is best. The Masai are famous for their dancing and bright red clothing.

# Herds and hunts

At the heart of the Rift Valley is the world-renowned Masai Mara. These vast grasslands teem with life. Herds of animals, including elephants and zebras, travel in search of vegetation and water. Hunters, such as cheetahs and lions, chase prey in pursuit of a meatier menu. Hungry hippos and crocodiles lurk in watering holes, and the Mara River, which flows through the reserve.

**Elephants ▶**
Herds of elephants travel to find water. Since they have no sweat glands, water keeps them cool.

**Wildebeest ▲**
Every year, thousands of wildebeest migrate from Tanzania to the Masai Mara in search of food and water.

**◀ Bateleur eagle**
This eagle, resting under a shady tree, spends eight hours a day in flight looking for food.

**▼ Warthogs**
By kneeling down, warthogs can eat the grass. Though normally peaceful, they will use their tusks if attacked.

**Honey badger ▼**
This badger tracks down food with its powerful sense of smell, even raiding the nests of birds and bees.

**Ground hornbill ▲**
This striking bird spends most of the time foraging for lizards, snakes, and spiders.

**◀ Cobra**
If under attack, this venomous snake assumes a threatening position and prepares to strike.

**▲ Slender mongooses**
Usually living alone or in pairs, slender mongooses hunt snakes, rodents, lizards, and birds.

**▲ Nile monitor lizard**
Africa's largest lizard is an able climber, with sharp claws and strong jaws. It lives near sources of water.

**◀ Lion**
A lion's mighty roar can be heard 5 miles (8 km) away. This huge cat feeds on large prey, such as buffalo.

**◄ White-backed vultures**
The white back of this vulture is only visible when it is in flight, scavenging for animal remains.

**Black rhinoceros ▼**
If a sudden noise or another animal disturbs a black rhinoceros it may charge at high speed.

**◄ Olive baboons**
Groups of olive baboons are led by a female. During the day, the group feeds together on vegetation.

**▼ Zebras**
For safety reasons, zebras drink in a group. Their stripes mingle, so predators struggle to single one out.

**▲ Giraffes**
One of the world's tallest animals, giraffes use their height to feed on the twigs and leaves of trees.

**Hyenas ▲**
These fast-moving hunters have extremely strong jaws that can bite through bone.

**▼ Nile crocodile**
At 16 ft (5 m) in length, this scaly hunter can leap suddenly from the water to catch a zebra or big cat.

**Impalas ▼**
These agile, African antelopes are hunted by every large predator in the Masai Mara.

**Cheetah ▲**
Hunting at speeds of up to 70 mph (110 kph), the cheetah is the fastest animal on land.

**◄ Oxpeckers**
These birds feed by perching on large mammals and pecking the bugs and ticks living in the fur.

**▲ Ostriches**
Although ostriches are the largest birds in the world, they cannot fly. Instead, they run very quickly.

**◄ Buffalo**
Weighing up to 2,000 lb (900 kg), bulky buffalo are more agile than they look and can even sprint.

# Grass roots

Lots of predators hunt in the Rift Valley, but fundamentally, all the animals depend on plants. Grass feeds the antelopes that lions and other hunters chase, while elephants and giraffes munch their way through the leaves and seeds of acacia trees. The flat-topped acacias also support wildlife in other ways—weaver birds build their nests in these trees and vicious ants live inside the thorns.

## How the rift formed

The Great Rift Valley is a giant geological fault that follows a line of weakness in Earth's crust. It began forming millions of years ago, and is still expanding today.

**1** The Rift started to form when Earth's crust began to pull in two different directions. Molten volcanic rock poured upward, and the surface started to break apart.

**2** As the crust separated, a huge slab of it sunk under its own weight, forming a valley with steep sides. Water flowed through the valley, creating rivers and lakes, and allowing grass to grow.

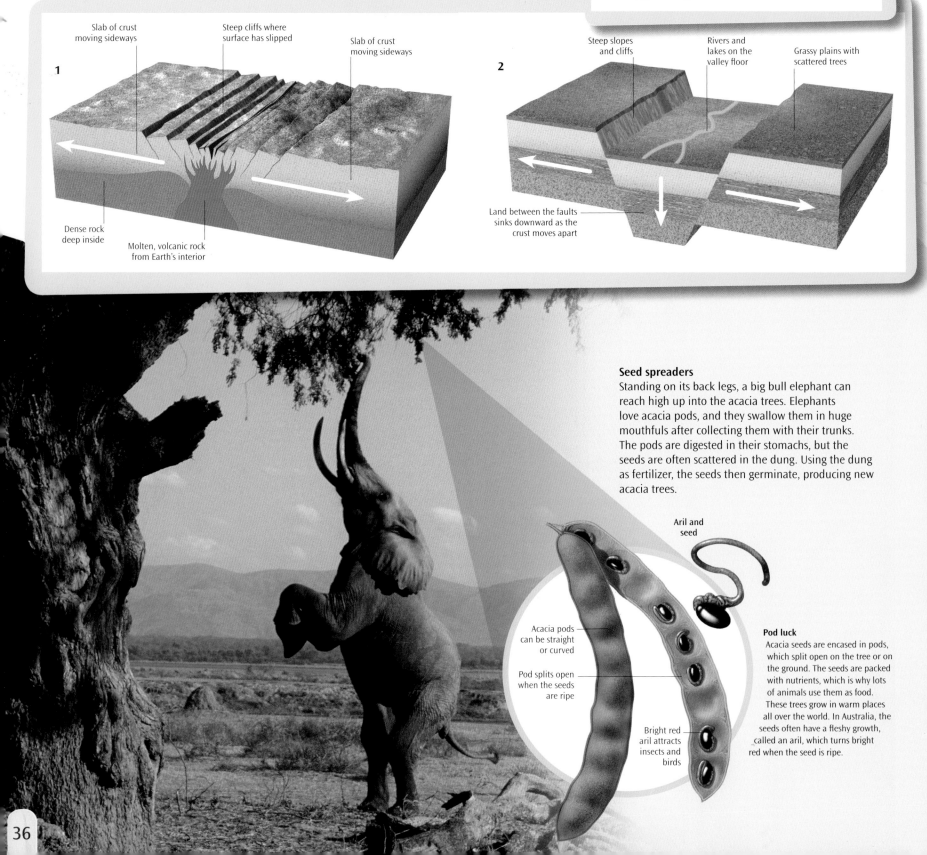

**1**

Slab of crust moving sideways

Steep cliffs where surface has slipped

Slab of crust moving sideways

Dense rock deep inside

Molten, volcanic rock from Earth's interior

**2**

Steep slopes and cliffs

Rivers and lakes on the valley floor

Grassy plains with scattered trees

Land between the faults sinks downward as the crust moves apart

## Seed spreaders

Standing on its back legs, a big bull elephant can reach high up into the acacia trees. Elephants love acacia pods, and they swallow them in huge mouthfuls after collecting them with their trunks. The pods are digested in their stomachs, but the seeds are often scattered in the dung. Using the dung as fertilizer, the seeds then germinate, producing new acacia trees.

Aril and seed

Acacia pods can be straight or curved

Pod splits open when the seeds are ripe

Bright red aril attracts insects and birds

## Pod luck

Acacia seeds are encased in pods, which split open on the tree or on the ground. The seeds are packed with nutrients, which is why lots of animals use them as food. These trees grow in warm places all over the world. In Australia, the seeds often have a fleshy growth, called an aril, which turns bright red when the seed is ripe.

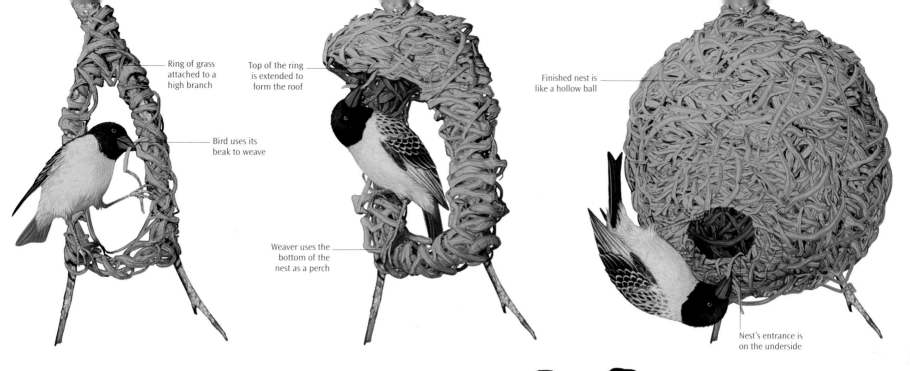

Ring of grass attached to a high branch

Top of the ring is extended to form the roof

Finished nest is like a hollow ball

Bird uses its beak to weave

Weaver uses the bottom of the nest as a perch

Nest's entrance is on the underside

## Working weavers

Weavers are seed-eating birds that make nests from leaves and grass. Each type of weaver has its own way of building its nest, but normally the male does the work. He starts by weaving a ring that is firmly attached to a branch, then he keeps weaving around it. Once the nest is finished, he waits for a female bird to move in.

## Caring crocodiles

Compared to most Rift Valley reptiles, crocodiles are very careful parents. They lay their eggs close to rivers or water holes and guard them until their young are about to hatch. When the baby crocodiles break out of their shells, the mother gently carries them in her jaws to the water.

## Tree trimmers

Giraffes eat the tasty leaves of acacia trees. Their tongues are long, and their lips are specially toughened to stop them from getting spiked by thorns. Over many years, giraffes trim away the branches, giving fully grown trees their distinctive flat-topped shape.

Base of thorn cut open to show nest inside

Sharp, hollow thorn

## Acacias and ants

Some of Africa's acacias have hollow swellings at the base of their thorns. These swellings are used as homes by acacia ants, who spend all their lives in trees. If an animal tries to eat the tree's leaves, the ants rush quickly from their nest and bite it—their way of paying the tree back for giving them a home.

Almost one million years ago, a new volcano burst its way through the floor of the Pacific Ocean. About 600,000 years later, it had grown so big that its red-hot lava started to emerge above the waves. Today, Mauna Loa towers over the island of Hawaii, measuring 29,500 ft (9,000 m) in height, from the top to the seabed. It is the world's largest active volcano, and the forested slopes are home to many rare animals and plants.

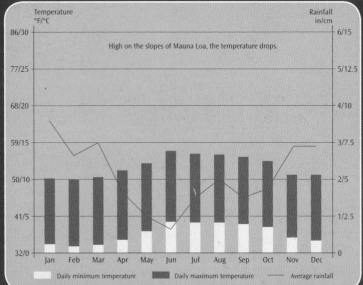

Kauai
Niihau
Oahu
Molokai
Lanai Maui
Kahoolawe
PACIFIC OCEAN
Hawaii    Mauna Loa

# Mauna Loa

## Cooling off

Temperature
°F/°C

Rainfall
in/cm

High on the slopes of Mauna Loa, the temperature drops.

| | 86/30 | | | | | | | | | | | 6/15 |
| 77/25 | | | | | | | | | | | 5/12.5 |
| 68/20 | | | | | | | | | | | 4/10 |
| 59/15 | | | | | | | | | | | 3/7.5 |
| 50/10 | | | | | | | | | | | 2/5 |
| 41/5 | | | | | | | | | | | 1/2.5 |
| 32/0 | Jan | Feb | Mar | Apr | May | Jun | Jul | Aug | Sep | Oct | Nov | Dec | 0 |

Daily minimum temperature          Daily maximum temperature          Average rainfall

**Rain catcher**
Although the Hawaiian Islands are famous for their sunny beaches, the eastern slopes of Mauna Loa are often shrouded in cloud and soaked with rain. Snow sometimes falls during the cold, winter months.

**The first Hawaiians**
The original inhabitants of the Hawaiian Islands were Polynesians—expert navigators who arrived by boat between 1,500 and 1,200 years ago. Today, Hawaii is a popular tourist destination, but some local fishermen still work from traditional canoes.

## Faces of the volcano

**Huge crater**
This aerial view of Mauna Loa shows its crater, which is nearly 3 miles (5 km) wide. It formed 1,000 years ago, when an eruption emptied lava at the summit. Once the lava drained away, the volcano's top caved in.

**Fast-flowing lava**
Despite its size, Mauna Loa is not one of the most dangerous volcanoes. Its lava is runny, rather than sticky, so it flows quickly downhill. This relieves the pressure inside the volcano, stopping it from blasting itself apart.

**Lava rock**
Once the lava cools, it turns into gray rock. In some places, the lava sets in jagged blocks, but in others it sets like smooth coils of rope. Hawaiians have their own names for these kinds of lava—a'a and pahoehoe.

**Nature's way**
Lava is packed with minerals that plants need to grow. On Mauna Loa's slopes, new lava fields are bare, but older ones are often covered with vegetation. Many plants that grow on the lava are found only on these islands.

**Hot spot**
Mauna Loa's last major eruption was in 1984. It was a spectacular sight, but no one was killed because the mountain's lava flows are highly visible and easy to escape from. However, during previous eruptions, lava has destroyed entire villages as it pours down the volcano's slopes.

**▼ 'Olapa**
Constantly fluttering leaves and great stature make the 'Olapa stand out in the Hawaiian forest.

**▼ Short-eared owl**
Hunting rodents by day, this silent flier is named after its two feather tufts that resemble ears.

**Hawaiian hawk ▼**
A territorial, lone bird with a shrill sound, this hawk feeds on insects and smaller birds.

**◄ Hawaiian crow**
A strong and fast flier, this noisy crow makes a loud, screeching call.

**◄ Hawaiian holly**
Reaching 60 ft (18 m) tall in rich soil, this common tree has smooth leaves and clusters of flowers.

**◄ Hawaiian thrush**
Known for its melodic song, this thrush is unusual because it shakes its wings while sitting.

**▲ Kakaemoa**
With its distinctive downward-pointing leaves, kakaemoa can grow as either a tree or a shrub.

**▼ Iiwi**
The long, curved beak of this songbird evolved from it regularly feeding on nectar inside flowers.

**Kamehameha butterfly ►**
One of only two types of butterfly native to these islands, the kamehameha feeds on tree sap.

**Mosquito ►**
The female of this tiny, flying insect drinks both blood and the nectar of flowering plants.

**◄ Feral pig**
This large pig with a big appetite eats a variety of forest food, such as roots, fruit, and plants.

**Polynesian rat ▼**
Active from dusk, this rodent eats insects, leaves, and worms. When food is limited, it even eats bark.

**▲ Hapu'u**
Hawaii's largest tree fern is unique to the islands, and can grow to 30 ft (9 m) in height.

# Protected land

The first settlers to Hawaii arrived in about AD 400. They introduced non-native animals to Mauna Loa, which disturbed the unique wildlife already living in the area and threatened the survival of certain species. In 1916, the Hawaii Volcanoes National Park was set up to preserve the native plants and animals. With a protected area of 505 sq miles (1,350 sq km), giant ferns, unusual flowers, and rare birds now flourish on the rich, volcanic land.

**Kauai** **Oahu** **Molokai** **Maui** **Niihau** **Lanai** **Kahoolawe** **Hawaii** **Hawaii Volcanoes National Park**

PACIFIC OCEAN

**Akiapolaau ▼**
Warbling away up in the trees, this bird looks for insects on branches and under bark.

**Apapane ▶**
A year-round singer, this bird prefers the nectar of the ohi'a flowers, but will eat insects, too.

**Acacia**
Preferring warm, wet climates, the large, thorny acacia is a fast-growing tree.

**Amakihi nest ▶**
Built from twigs, bark, and leaves, this tightly bound nest holds the amakihi chicks.

**▲ Ohi'a**
Features of this tree include dark wood, leaves of varying shapes and sizes, and nectar-filled flowers.

**◀ Amakihi**
In the honeycreeper family of birds, the amakihi enjoys sweet food, such as nectar and fruit.

**◀ Hawaiian hoary bats**
Roosting in the forest trees during the daylight hours, these bats fly at night, hunting insects to eat.

**▼ Uluhe**
Like a vine, uluhe winds around other plants as it grows, creating a dense forest floor of vegetation.

**▼ Mongooses**
Playful mongooses live in small groups and feed on snakes, rodents, and insects.

**▼ Carabid beetles**
Often called ground beetles, these shiny, long-legged bugs eat small or injured insects.

**Drosophila fly ▼**
In its courtship dance to attract a female, the male shifts from side to side and beats its patterned wings.

**Spider ▶**
Mauna Loa's spiders include native island species and ones that have been brought in from outside.

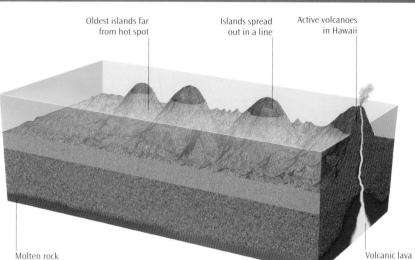

Oldest islands far from hot spot

Islands spread out in a line

Active volcanoes in Hawaii

Molten rock

Volcanic lava rising from hot spot

# Lava living

It takes hundreds of years for plants to cover a lava flow completely. Once the lava has cooled and turned solid, ferns start to grow, and the steel gray surface becomes covered in greenery. After these pioneers have arrived, other plants move in slowly, and animals follow. But it's a delicate process, and it is easily upset by intruders that have been accidentally or deliberately brought in from outside the area. That is why many of Mauna Loa's plants and animals now depend on conservation to survive.

**How the Hawaiian Islands formed**
The islands were created by a volcanic "hot spot," under the Pacific Ocean. Over millions of years, the ocean floor has slid westward over the hot spot, creating a row of islands. Hawaii is currently over the hot spot. Millions of years from now, another island will take its place.

**The lucky few**
Ferns don't have flowers. Instead, they make their spores in small pouches on the underside of their fronds (leaves). A single fern can make more than a billion spores every year. But only a tiny number are lucky enough to land in damp, shady cracks, where they can start to grow.

**Pioneering plants**
Ferns are often the first plants to set up home on Hawaii's bare lava flows. They grow in cracks, where there is moisture and protection from the bright sunshine. Ferns are good at spreading. Instead of growing seeds, they produce microscopic spores, which blow far and wide on the wind.

Fern fronds unroll as they grow

Spores drift away in the air

Outer covering or spore pouch

Spores released into the air

Capsules on narrow stalk

**Spore production**
This is the inside of a spore pouch, magnified hundreds of times. The spores are made in tiny capsules, which split open when they are ripe. Ferns have complicated life cycles. When a fern spore germinates, it produces a flat plant no bigger than a stamp. This plant eventually withers away, and a new adult fern plant takes its place.

# Great Barrier Reef

The biggest structure ever built by living things is the Great Barrier Reef. Off the northeast coast of Australia, the reef covers 131,000 sq miles (340,000 sq km), and weighs billions of tons. It is a collection of many thousands of reefs, set in the clear, blue waters of the Coral Sea. Despite its gigantic size, this natural wonder is made up of tiny marine creatures. Their dead skeletons have piled up over thousands of years, creating the reef that exists today.

PAPUA NEW GUINEA

Solomon Sea

SOLOMON ISLANDS

Torres Strait

Great Barrier Reef

Coral Sea

VANUATU

Queensland

AUSTRALIA

NEW CALEDONIA (To France)

New South Wales

Tasman Sea

## Exploring the reef

**Idyllic islands**
Thousands of islands are scattered along the reef. Some are covered with lush vegetation, while others, known as cays, are bare expanses of brilliant white coral sand. At high tide, some cays disappear entirely.

**Channels and creeks**
In parts of the reef, deep water channels and creeks look like rivers between the coral. These channels are now carefully mapped, but when Europeans first explored the reef, ships were often wrecked.

**Outer reef**
On its seaward edge, the reef is pounded by large waves rolling in from the open ocean. Beneath the surface, the reef drops like a cliff into deep water, creating a feeding ground for big fish, such as sharks.

**Inner reef**
Sheltered from the waves, the inner reef is calm. The water here is often shallow, with scattered coral gardens separated by open areas of sand. At low tide, the fragile tips of the corals may be exposed.

**▲ Sunlight**
As the Sun's rays warm the reef, the water temperature rarely drops below 70°F (22°C).

**▲ Bottlenose dolphins**
Traveling in playful pods, these strong swimmers fish near the surface of the water.

**◄ Lionfish**
With its poisonous spines and large fins, a lionfish traps its prey quickly and swallows it whole.

**▲ Rocks**
Large, granite rocks lie on the seabed, and marine plants often grow from their tough surfaces.

**Gorgonian sea fans ►**
Attaching themselves to sand, the sea fan's treelike tentacles wave around to catch tiny animals.

**▲ Sea star**
If one of its arms gets severed, a blue sea star can produce a whole new body from the base.

**◄ Flatworms**
About 20,000 species make up the flatworm family. They can be microscopic or 3 ft (1 m) long.

**▲ Large star coral**
An important reef-builder, this large coral grows in huge colonies all over the reef.

# Underwater world

Palm Island is a beach paradise off the northeast coast of Australia. In 1770, the explorer Captain Cook gave the island its name when he saw palm trees growing there. Beneath these sandy shores, a diverse range of aquatic inhabitants live in the clear, warm waters. Seagrass, sponges, and starfish make a spectacular seabed. Sharks and turtles swim over colorful coral and clams, while shoals of fish and pods of dolphins dart around the reef.

**PAPUA NEW GUINEA**
**SOLOMON ISLANDS**
*Solomon Sea*
*Torres Strait*
*Great Barrier Reef*
*Coral Sea*
**VANUATU**
**Palm Island Group**
**QUEENSLAND**
**NEW CALEDONIA** (To France)
**AUSTRALIA**
**New South Wales**
*Tasman Sea*

**▼ Sea whips**
The structure of this coral is very simple. It is straight, has no branches, and grows in colonies.

**◀ Green turtle**
One of the largest marine turtles, this heavyweight swimmer is named after its green-colored fat.

**▲ Red-bellied fusiliers**
Growing to a maximum length of 10 in (25 cm), these schools of fish seek shelter in coral or rocks.

**Crown-of-thorns starfish ▲**
Covered in spiny thorns to protect itself, this starfish feeds on coral and prefers sheltered waters.

**Spotted reef crab ▶**
The aptly named spotted reef crab has big pincers to scavenge for plants and dead fish.

**Banded goby ▲**
Tranquil by nature, the banded goby prefers to swim in still water just above the sand.

**Seagrass ▲**
One of the few flowering plants that lives in the sea, seagrass covers large expanses of the reef.

**Lava tubes**
Hidden under the ground in the Hawaiian Islands are lava tubes—giant caves that look like corridors. They were created by rivers of lava flowing downhill. The outside cooled and hardened, but the inside stayed hot and runny, leaving behind a hollow tube. One of Mauna Loa's lava tubes stretches almost 30 miles (50 km) from the mountain to the sea. It formed after a huge eruption more than a century ago.

## Unwelcome intruders

**Feral pigs**
Polynesian seafarers brought pigs to the islands more than 1,500 years ago. Since then, many have escaped and now live in the wild. These pigs root up many of the endangered plants and remove soil by churning up the ground.

**Rats**
In the days of wooden ships, rats were common stowaways. Over the centuries, many of them scuttled ashore. They have spread all over the islands, raiding the nests of birds to steal their eggs and chicks.

**Wild dogs**
Packs of wild dogs are a problem for some of the rarest animals, including the Hawaiian goose—the islands' state bird. As Hawaiian geese nest on the ground, it is easy for dogs to track them down and attack.

**Argentine ants**
Before people arrived, there were no ants on the islands. Today, there are at least 40 kinds. The Argentine ant is one of the smallest, but it causes a problem by taking food needed by Hawaii's own insects.

## Under threat

**Laysan ducks**
This rare duck lives on Laysan Island, at the west end of the island chain. After rabbits were released on Laysan, the duck numbers dwindled to just 33 by the 1950s. Thanks to conservation work, there are now 500 ducks.

**Mauna kea silverswords**
The silversword has furry leaves and grows near the summit of Mauna Loa. Goats and sheep eat this plant, so hundreds of silverswords have been fenced off to keep these animals away.

**Koa bugs**
Once a common sight throughout the Hawaiian Islands, this insect is disappearing fast. No one knows exactly why, but some scientists think it might be a victim of parasitic insects, which have accidentally entered the islands.

**Akiapolaaus**
This forest bird has been hit by avian (bird) malaria—a disease carried by mosquitoes. Before people arrived, the islands had no mosquitoes or malaria, so Hawaiian birds do not have any resistance to the disease.

## A shifting landscape

**Quiver trees**
The spiky quiver is one of the few trees that can survive here. They grow up to 26 ft (8 m) tall, and have thick water-storing trunks. Hunters use the bark to make quivers (arrow-holders), which is how the trees got their name.

**Grassy plains**
Farther inland, there is enough moisture for grass to grow. Antelopes, herds of cattle, and about 2,500 cheetahs live on the grassy plains. A conservation program helps to protect these endangered cats.

**Skeleton Coast**
With its currents, fog, and shifting sands, this coastline is hazardous for shipping. The shore is dotted with the rusty remains of ships that ran aground. The coast is named after the large number of lives it has claimed.

**Ancient mountains**
In Namibia's interior, mountain ranges have been eroded into eye-catching shapes. Snakes, baboons, and antelopes live in these mountains. In the summer, the rock is too hot for climbers to scale.

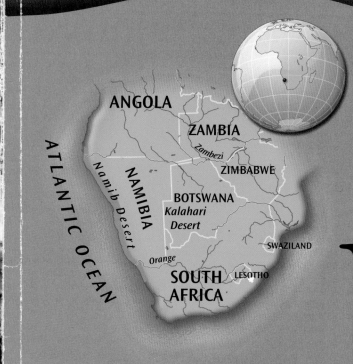

ANGOLA
ZAMBIA
*Zambezi*
ZIMBABWE
*Namib Desert*
NAMIBIA
BOTSWANA
*Kalahari Desert*
ATLANTIC OCEAN
SWAZILAND
*Orange*
SOUTH AFRICA
LESOTHO

Many deserts are bigger than the Namib in Africa, but few can match its amazing scenery or its strange wildlife. The Namib has some of the world's highest sand dunes, which stretch inland from the wild and desolate Atlantic coast. A fog rolls in from the ocean every night, carrying moisture that helps to keep the desert's plants and animals alive.

# Namib Desert

**Barracudas ▶**
Suddenly swimming at speed, barracudas catch prey using their strong jaws and fangs.

**▼ Blacktip reef shark**
A common sight on the reef, this shark can be 6 ft (2m) in length. It swims alone, hunting fish.

**▲ Manta ray**
The largest of the ray family, the agile manta can leap clean out of the water.

**▼ Crimson soldierfish**
Usually found in the reef's small caves and crevices, these fish come out to feed in large schools.

**▼ Wobbegong**
This well camouflaged shark stays on the seabed in order to avoid predators and to surprise prey.

**Coral ▶**
The skeletons of tiny marine life build up over time to create hard deposits of coral, which form a reef.

**▼ Pearl-scaled angelfish**
Growing to a maximum length of 5 in (12 cm), this smooth swimmer feeds on sponges.

**Spanish dancer ▲**
A large nudibranch (sea slug without a shell), the Spanish dancer moves by rising and falling in waves.

**▼ Golden butterfly fish**
Shy by nature, the golden butterfly
fish eats worms on the seabed and
insects near the surface of the water.

**▼ Yellowfin parrotfish**
With teeth similar to a parrot's beak,
parrotfish graze on coral by day
and sleep on the seabed at night.

**Cuttlefish ▲**
Nicknamed the "sea chameleon,"
the cuttlefish can change its skin
color to hide from predators.

**Striped cleaner wrasse ▶**
Setting up "cleaning stations,"
wrasse pick off the parasites
found on passing larger fish
and eat them.

**Narrow-lined pufferfish ▼**
When under threat, the puffer
family of fish can inflate
themselves quickly so they
look too big to eat.

**▲ Barred spinefoot**
If under threat, this fish can
raise its venomous spines
quickly to deter an attack.

**Fan worms ▶**
Nicknamed feather duster worms,
fan worms drain water through
their fans to collect tiny marine life.

**Sea anemones ▶**
Attached to rocks by a suckerlike
disk, the anemone catches tiny
food in its stinging tentacles.

**Pink anemonefish ▲**
These fish live among the sea
anemone's tentacles. In return
for food scraps, they clean
the anemone.

**◄ Sea urchins**
Resembling prickly hedgehogs,
these spiny marine creatures
move slowly along the seabed.

**▲ Topshells**
Recognizable by their cone shape,
topshells rest on the rocks and
feed on miniature aquatic plants.

## Tropical temperatures

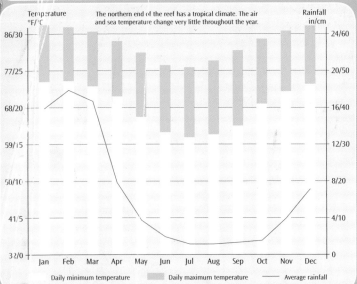

The northern end of the reef has a tropical climate. The air and sea temperature change very little throughout the year.

| Temperature °F/°C | | Rainfall in/cm |
|---|---|---|

Temperature scale: 86/30, 77/25, 68/20, 59/15, 50/10, 41/5, 32/0

Rainfall scale: 24/60, 20/50, 16/40, 12/30, 8/20, 4/10, 0

Months: Jan Feb Mar Apr May Jun Jul Aug Sep Oct Nov Dec

Daily minimum temperature — Daily maximum temperature — Average rainfall

### Coral bleaching
Reef-building corals cannot grow in cold water, but very warm water also harms them. If the sea temperature rises above about 86°F (30ºC), corals turn white and often die. This problem is called coral bleaching.

### Divers' paradise
Armed with a spotlight, a diver investigates the outer reef. This area attracts thousands of visitors every year, so it must be protected. Special regulations control where people can dive, fish, and anchor boats, to reduce coral damage.

### ...n divide
...reat Barrier Reef forms a natural barrier between ...ast and the open ocean, which is how it got its ... Most of the reef is more than 50 miles (80 km) ...it cannot be seen from the shore. However, it is ...us enough to be clearly seen from space.

## Fog-covered desert

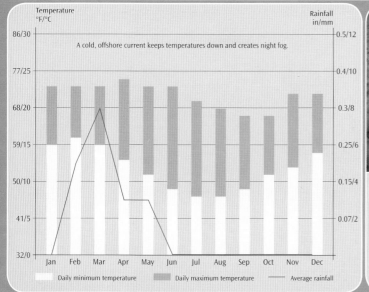

Temperature
°F/°C

Rainfall
in/mm

A cold, offshore current keeps temperatures down and creates night fog.

86/30 · · · 0.5/12
77/25 · · · 0.4/10
68/20 · · · 0.3/8
59/15 · · · 0.25/6
50/10 · · · 0.15/4
41/5 · · · 0.07/2
32/0

Jan Feb Mar Apr May Jun Jul Aug Sep Oct Nov Dec

Daily minimum temperature      Daily maximum temperature      Average rainfall

**Minimal moisture**
About every 10 years, enough rain falls in the Namib to create temporary pools. However, near the coast, the only reliable moisture comes from sea fog. It rolls in every night, before the sun burns it away after dawn.

**Native Namibians**
The Herero and Himba are two closely related groups of native Namibians. Traditionally, they live by herding cattle—a tough job in the region's extremely dry climate. Men usually look after the herds, while women milk the animals. Himba women decorate their skin with ocher (a red powder) mixed with butter fat.

**Black-breasted snake eagle ▶**
Named after its taste for snakes, this eagle will also eat lizards and small birds when food is scarce.

**Leopard ▼**
Usually a night stalker, the leopard will take daylight opportunities to hunt, if it spots prey nearby.

**▼ Aardwolf**
With its long, sticky tongue, the lone aardwolf can eat thousands of insects every day.

**▼ Brown hyena**
Whether it is melon or antelope, the hyena's powerful sense of smell can detect food easily.

**Nara plant ▼**
Native to the Namib, this spiny bush produces melons, which are eaten by many desert creatures.

**Cape fox ▲**
In the day, the small, agile cape fox keeps cool under a tree or in a rocky den. It hunts after the Sun sets.

**Chacma baboons ▶**
One of the largest monkeys, these baboons live in playful family groups called troops.

**Cape hare ▼**
Desert shrubs contain moisture, so when the cape hare eats them, it gets enough food and water to survive.

**Secretary bird ▶**
The long legs of the secretary bird can stamp and kill prey, such as snakes, other reptiles, and rodents.

**Ludwig's bustard ▲**
Although this bird is a strong flier, it prefers to stay on the ground and use its long legs for running.

**◀ Mountain wheatear**
Building its nest on rocky ground, this insect-eater sings sweet-sounding tunes.

**Lappet-faced vulture ▶**
A dominant desert bird, this huge vulture is often first at the scene when there is a carcass to feed on.

**Cartwheel spider ▶**
By rolling down the dunes, this spider can save energy and escape predators quickly.

**Namibian edelweiss ▲**
Edelweiss grows in remote places, and it stands out because the flowers and leaves are coated in white hairs.

**Gemsbok ▲**
A long-horned African antelope, gemsbok travel in small herds and eat melons for their water content.

**◄ Camelthorn tree**
During the hottest part of the day, tired animals gather under this thorny tree to lie in the shade.

**◄ Ostriches**
Weighing up to 330 lb (150 kg), these big birds get the water they need from the plants they eat.

**Springbok ▲**
One of the antelope family's smaller members, springbok sprint, jump, and play together.

**Peringuey's adder ▶**
A small, venomous viper, this snake lies in wait under the sand before ambushing its prey.

**▼ Olive whipsnake**
Named after its long, whiplike tail, this fast-moving snake can climb trees to escape attackers.

**Caracal ▶**
This cat can survive for long periods without water and jump 10 ft (3 m) to catch a bird in flight.

**▼ Grant's golden mole burrow**
Sand collapses as the golden mole digs underground, so its burrows are always temporary.

**▼ Darkling beetle**
In the midday sun, this beetle cools off by burrowing into the sand or running fast to make a breeze.

# Dune-dwellers

ANGOLA
ZAMBIA
Zambezi
ZIMBABWE
ATLANTIC OCEAN
Namib Desert
NAMIBIA
BOTSWANA
Kalahari Desert
Sossusvlei
SWAZILAND
Orange
SOUTH AFRICA
LESOTHO

The highest sand dunes in the world can be found in Sossusvlei, an area in the south of the Namib. Although this hot, hostile land appears desolate, a surprising amount of wildlife can survive here. By adapting to the environment and finding sources of food and water in unexpected places, a variety of animals, insects, and plants overcome the difficulties of desert life.

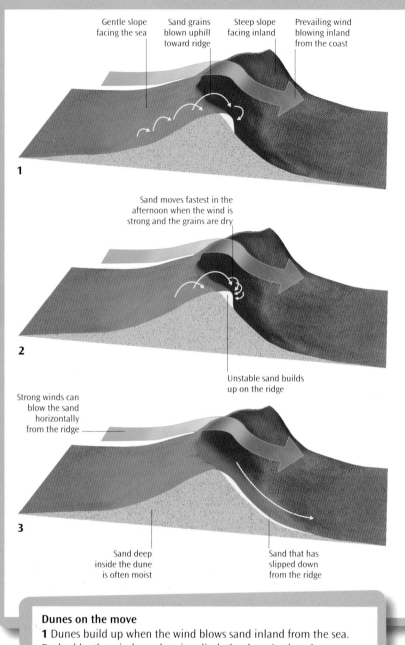

Gentle slope facing the sea

Sand grains blown uphill toward ridge

Steep slope facing inland

Prevailing wind blowing inland from the coast

**1**

Sand moves fastest in the afternoon when the wind is strong and the grains are dry

**2**

Unstable sand builds up on the ridge

Strong winds can blow the sand horizontally from the ridge

**3**

Sand deep inside the dune is often moist

Sand that has slipped down from the ridge

**Dunes on the move**

**1** Dunes build up when the wind blows sand inland from the sea. Pushed by the wind, sand grains climb the dune in short hops, and pile up on the crest of the ridge.

**2** More and more sand builds up on the crest, creating a very steep slope just below the ridge. The sand becomes more and more unstable, and a single footstep can make it give way.

**3** Suddenly, the sand breaks loose, and moves down the slope. Each time this happens, the dune moves a short distance farther inland. Meanwhile, new dunes form near the shore.

Fog condenses on the beetle's body

Water drop hanging from beetle's head

# Sand survival

The Namib's dunes have lots of different shapes, and they are always on the move. For people, climbing them is hard work, but the desert's animals take it in their stride. Geckos and beetles scuttle over the sand, while sidewinding adders throw themselves forward like someone flicking a rope. The golden mole has its own solution to the mobility problem. It swims beneath the surface, like a submarine in a sandy sea.

Tracks left by the sidewinder

**Sidewinders**

Most snakes slither across the ground, but in the Namib, one kind of snake has a very different method of moving. The Peringuey's adder throws itself sideways through the air, leaving a row of tracks on the dunes. Sidewinding is an efficient way of moving across sand, and it also helps to keep the snake cool. Peringuey's adder is not the only snake that moves like this. In the deserts of North America, the sidewinder rattlesnake crosses sandy ground in the same way.

Between tracks, the sidewinder leaps in the air

Ridge of sand shows where the mole has been burrowing

## Drinking fog

The darkling beetle has a very unusual way of getting a drink. It climbs the dunes after dark, and then stands on the crest, with its back tilted upward and toward the wind. When the sea fog rolls inland, it condenses on the beetle's body. Small droplets run down the beetle's body to its mouth, quenching its thirst.

## Different dunes

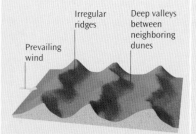

Steep slope | Small barchans move faster than large ones
Prevailing wind

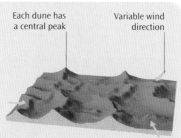

Irregular ridges | Deep valleys between neighboring dunes
Prevailing wind

Each dune has a central peak | Variable wind direction

### Barchan dunes

From the air, barchan dunes are shaped like a letter "C." The ends of the C point away from the wind, and lead the way as the dune moves. These dunes can be 330 ft (100 m) from end to end.

### Transverse dunes

These dunes are arranged in parallel rows, at right angles to the wind. Unlike barchan dunes, they move slowly, but they can be more than 30 miles (50 km) in length.

### Star dunes

The tallest dunes of all, these form when the wind blows in different directions, piling the sand into giant heaps. Star dunes have complicated outlines, with many ridges and slopes.

## Underground attack

The golden mole feeds on geckos and termites by grabbing them from below. As it burrows through the sand, it stops and listens for the sound of its prey moving overhead. If something comes within range, the mole suddenly bursts through the sand and catches it with razor-sharp teeth.

Web-footed gecko looks for insects on the dunes

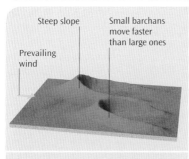

## Flower feeding

Humans are not alone in enjoying sweet drinks. In the Namib, sunbirds drink sugary nectar from aloe flowers, a family of plants that includes the quiver tree. The beaks of the sunbirds are long and curved—just the right shape for reaching deep inside a flower, to where the nectar is produced.

Fur covers the tiny eyes

Burrow fills in as the mole moves on

As the highest mountain in the world, Mount Everest puts its neighboring peaks in the shade. Its summit is 29,028 ft (8,848 m) high—almost the cruising altitude for passenger planes! The upper slopes are permanently covered in ice and snow, and often blasted by winds of more than 125 mph (200 kph). Everest was first climbed in 1953. Since then, hundreds of climbers have reached the top, although not all of them have returned to tell the tale.

# Mount Everest

**The roof of the world**

Mount Everest is in the Himalayas, the world's highest mountain chain. The Himalayas are spread across eight countries and include all of the world's top 100 highest mountains. Due to their jagged peaks and steep sides, some of the mountains nearby are even harder to climb than Mount Everest itself.

## Peak condition

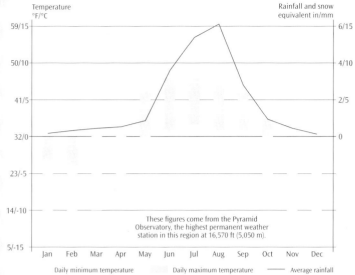

| Temperature °F/°C | | Rainfall and snow equivalent in/mm |
|---|---|---|
| 59/15 | | 6/15 |
| 50/10 | | 4/10 |
| 41/5 | | 2/5 |
| 32/0 | | 0 |
| 23/-5 | | |
| 14/-10 | | |
| 5/-15 | | |

These figures come from the Pyramid Observatory, the highest permanent weather station in this region at 16,570 ft (5,050 m).

Jan  Feb  Mar  Apr  May  Jun  Jul  Aug  Sep  Oct  Nov  Dec

Daily minimum temperature      Daily maximum temperature      — Average rainfall

### Blizzard warning
Mount Everest is in Asia's monsoon climate zone. The worst blizzards are during the monsoon season, which lasts from June to October. The best time for climbing Mount Everest is in April and May, before the monsoon starts.

### Mountain sherpas
Sherpas are the local people living on the Nepali side of Mount Everest. They traditionally live by farming and raising cattle, but some also work as guides and porters. In 1953, a Sherpa named Tenzing Norgay became the joint first man to stand on the summit, with his fellow climber Edmund Hillary.

## Scenes from the slopes

### Space shot
From space, Mount Everest looks like a three-sided pyramid. The peak itself is on the border between Nepal and China. Most climbers use the southeast ridge, which snakes its way up on the Nepali side.

### The summit
Winds at the summit of Mount Everest create a plume of ice crystals that is visible from far away. The wind piles up the snow on dangerous overhangs, which can break without warning under a climber's weight.

### Khumbu Icefall
Climbers making their way up Mount Everest from Nepal must cross the Khumbu Icefall. This notoriously difficult part of the Khumbu Glacier is riddled with chasms and loose blocks of ice bigger than a house.

### Valleys and foothills
At the base of Mount Everest, fast-flowing rivers rush through deep valleys. In the foothills, these valleys are covered in lush vegetation and wildlife—a contrast to the bleak conditions at the top.

# High life

The world's highest national park is Sagarmatha in Nepal—the home of Mount Everest. Forests of pine and hemlock line the lower slopes, where many types of birds and butterflies seek shelter from the cold. Thick fur helps the larger animals keep warm, including the endangered snow leopard, red panda, and Himalayan black bear.

▲ **Snow leopard**
Living high in the mountains, this big cat can leap about 30 ft (9 m)!

▲ **Himalayan griffon**
This scavenger with a big appetite looks out for the remains of a kill, then swoops down to feast.

▼ **Himalayan tahr**
A tahr's thick, furry undercoat and strong, flexible hooves are suited to the cold, rocky habitat.

▼ **Birch rhododendron**
Dense birch rhododendron trees crowd the alpine slopes, interspersed with ferns and mosses.

▲ **Snow pigeons**
Native to the Himalayas, flocks of these pigeons fly high over the mountains.

▲ **Lammergeier**
With a wingspan up to 10 ft (3 m), the lammergeier can float on rising currents of air.

▼ **Fir trees**
Usually found at high altitude, fir trees have cones that close in the cold and open when it is warmer.

**Himalayan black bear** ▼
Excellent sight, hearing, and smell help the solitary black bear find food in the thick undergrowth.

CHINA

Himalayas

NEPAL

BHUTAN

Sagarmatha National Park

Brahmaputra

Ganges River

MYANMAR (BURMA)

BANGLADESH

INDIA

Bay of Bengal

**▼ Gray wolf**
Wolves howl to warn off other packs. Their call can be heard 6 miles (10 km) away.

**◄ Hemlock trees**
This large, evergreen tree with flat leaves and small cones thrives in damp places.

**▼ Indian muntjac**
To mark its territory, the muntjac rubs the "V" shape scent glands on its head against foliage.

**▼ Himalayan weasel**
This active weasel lives alone, and hunts small birds and rodents by day and night.

**▼ Rhododendron campanulatum**
These bell-shaped flowers bloom in the spring. However, the tough, evergreen leaves are poisonous.

**◄ Civet**
A relative of the mongoose family, the speedy civet lives in dense woodland and eats meat and fruit.

**Common rat ▶**
There is a big rat population here, thanks to the rodent's breeding rate, varied diet, and sharp senses.

**▼ Tibetan water shrew**
Small and secretive, this shrew scours mountain streams for insects to eat.

**▼ Red panda**
A member of the racoon family, the red panda can eat up to half its body weight in leaves each day.

**Blood pheasant ▲**
The eye-catching male blood pheasant uses its colorful feathers to attract a mate.

**Common red apollo ▲**
Flying at high altitude, the apollo butterfly stops to sip nectar from the mountain flowers.

# Adapting to altitude

Life is hard high up in the Himalayas. Without special adaptations and strategies, animals would soon die from hunger or from the cold. For birds such as the lammergeier—a giant bone-breaking vulture—the mountain slopes provide an ideal feeding ground. Like other Himalayan animals, it is well protected against the low temperatures and lives in a location where there are few people and lots of room to roam.

**60 million years ago**

Indian plate

Ocean separating Indian plate from Eurasian plate

Volcanoes form where plates collide

Indian plate forced downward

Eurasian plate

**30 million years ago**

Ocean has narrowed and then disappeared

Indian plate and Eurasian plate join to form a single landmass

Indian plate driven underneath Eurasian plate

**Today**

Himalayan Plateau

Himalayas are continually being forced upward

Earthquakes are triggered by the collision of the two plates

Claws are used to grip bones

Legs covered in feathers

### How the Himalayas formed

The Himalayas began to form about 60 million years ago, when two parts of the Earth's crust were on a collision course. One of them—the Indian plate—moved north toward the much bigger Eurasian plate. The ocean between them steadily narrowed, and eventually disappeared. In the collision, the Indian plate was driven underneath the Eurasian plate, pushing up the Himalayas. Today, the Indian plate is still forcing its way north at a rate of about 2 in (5 cm) a year.

### Bone breakers

The lammergeier soars over the mountain slopes. It feeds on the tough parts of dead animals, and has a special technique for getting at the juicy marrow inside bones. It picks up bones and then drops them from a great height, so that they smash apart on the rocks below.

## Top cats

Snow leopards live at altitudes of up to 20,000 ft (6,000 m)—higher than any other big cat. Their fur is thick and warm, and its pale color helps to hide them when they hunt in the snow. With their unusually long tails and furry, padded paws, they can wrap up snugly when they lie down to sleep.

Wing feathers spread apart, helping the vulture to soar

## Making hay

Unlike most vultures, this bird has a feathery head to keep it warm

Feathery beard on each side of beak

Bone cracked open revealing the marrow

The same rocks are often used year after year

Pikas are small mammals belonging to the rabbit family, although they look more like a rodent with large ears. They live in rocky crevices and survive the winter by collecting plants and drying them like hay. Pikas often collect more than they can eat—a useful precaution in case the winter turns out to be unusually long or hard.

# Glossary

**Abdomen**
The rear part of an insect's body. In some insects, it ends in a sting.

**Adapting**
Changing in shape or behavior to suit new ways of life. All living things adapt, but it is a very slow process that can take hundreds or thousands of years.

**Antenna (pl. antennae)**
An animal's feelers. Insects have two antennae, but some other animals have four.

**Barrier reef**
A long coral reef separated from the coast by open water or a lagoon.

**Camouflage**
Having colors and patterns that blend in with the background and work as a disguise.

**Canopy**
The thick layer of leaves and branches in a forest, high above the ground.

**Carnivorous**
Anything that eats animals as food. Most carnivorous animals are hunters, but some scavenge food from dead remains.

**Cay**
A low island made of coral sand. Cays are often flooded by the sea at high tide.

**Channel**
A narrow stretch of water.

**Chasm**
A deep cleft in the Earth's surface, or a large hollow space underground.

**Cocoon**
A silk case made by an insect or a spider. Insect grubs shut themselves inside cocoons so that they can change into adults.

**Condense**
Changing from a vapor into a liquid. Water vapor in the air condenses to make droplets of dew.

**Conservation**
Processes that help to protect natural habitats and safeguard wild plants and animals. Conservation work is carried out in many different ways—in the wild, as well as in research centers and zoos.

**Coral**
A small sea animal that often lives inside a hard case. Over many years, these cases can build up to make coral reefs.

**Coral bleaching**
A process that makes coral turn white. Coral bleaching happens when the sea around coral reefs gets too warm.

**Crater**
A bowl-shaped hollow high up on a volcano, created by an eruption. Craters can also be caused by meteorites hitting Earth from space.

**Creek**
A narrow inlet of the sea.

**Crust**
Earth's hard outer surface. The crust includes all the continents and the rocks under the seabed.

**Dam**
Something that blocks a river, making water build up behind it to form a lake. Dams are built to store water, and to drive turbines that make electricity.

**Endangered**
A word used to describe any living thing that is disappearing fast and at risk of becoming extinct.

**Erosion**
Anything that wears down rock, or that breaks it into smaller pieces. Erosion can be caused by many things, including glaciers, rivers, waves, and wind.

**Evergreen**
A plant that keeps its leaves all year round. Most of the trees in tropical rain forests are evergreen, as are most conifers, such as firs and pines.

**Extinct**
A word used for plants or animals that have completely died out.

**Feral**
An animal that has escaped and taken up life in the wild.

**Fjord**
A deep valley that has been gouged out by a glacier, and then flooded due to a rise in the sea level.

**Geological fault**
Where stress in Earth's crust is released, a fault line occurs. This is often associated with earthquakes.

**Glacier**
A large river of slowly moving ice. The ice moves downhill under its own weight.

**Gorge**
A narrow valley with steep sides. Gorges are made when rivers slowly carve their way through soft rocks.

**Grazer**
A large animal that feeds mainly on grass. Grazers include antelopes, zebras, and cattle.

**Grub**
A young insect without wings, and sometimes without legs.

**Hanging valley**
A side valley that ends high up above a main valley. Hanging valleys are made by glaciers.

**Hot spring**
A place where volcanically heated water gushes out of the ground.

**Ice cap**
A huge layer of ice that completely covers the land underneath.

**Ice floe**
A large piece of ice floating on the surface of the sea. Unlike icebergs, ice floes form at sea, when the sea's surface freezes.

**Ice shelf**
A glacier that stretches far out to sea.

**Iceberg**
A large chunk of ice that has broken off from a glacier and floated out to sea.

**Incubate**
Sitting on eggs and keeping them warm until they hatch.

**Kopje**
A pile of large rocks and boulders surrounded by grassland.

**Larva (pl. larvae)**
A young insect that changes shape to become an adult. Unlike adult insects, larvae never have wings.

**Lava**
The hot molten rock that pours out of volcanoes.

**Lava flow**
A river of lava that pours down the slopes of a volcano.

**Lichen**
A living thing that resembles a plant and grows on rocks or trees. Lichens are a mixture of two different partners—a fungus and a microscopic alga.

**Limestone**
A rock that is often made from tiny pieces of shell or minerals, which have settled on the seabed and then solidified.

**Migration**
Long journeys undertaken by animals. Animals migrate so that they can avoid cold winters and raise their young where there is plenty of food.

**Mineral**
Substances that make up rocks.

**Monsoon**
In the tropics, a season of the year when it rains heavily almost every day. The monsoon starts when the wind changes and blows clouds inland from the sea.

**Parasite**
An animal that lives on or in another animal and uses it to get food. Parasites are usually much smaller than the animals that they live on.

**Plate**
A huge piece of the Earth's crust. The planet's entire surface is divided into plates. All of them are slowly on the move, driven by volcanic heat.

**Plateau**
A high, flat plain.

**Predator**
Any animal that catches and kills other animals for food. Most predators chase other animals one by one but some predators, such as whales, scoop up their prey in large amounts.

**Prey**
An animal that is caught and eaten by a predator. Many prey animals feed on plants alone, but some are predators themselves.

**Rain forest**
A forest where it rains heavily all year round. Most rain forests are in the tropics, but they also grow on coasts in colder parts of the world.

**Reef**
Outcrops of rocks or corals that lie close to the surface of the sea.

**Rift valley**
A huge, trenchlike valley formed where the Earth's crust has split apart.

**Sandstone**
A type of rock made of small grains of sand that have become glued together firmly.

**Scent glands**
Special organs in animals that release substances with a lingering smell. Animals use these scents to find each other, to ward off predators, and to mark territories.

**Schist**
A kind of rock that splits easily into flakes or bigger slabs.

**Sedimentary rock**
Any rock that has formed from small particles of sediment or from fossil material. Common sedimentary rocks include sandstone, limestone, and shale.

**Shale**
A type of rock made from tiny particles of mud or clay that have settled out in water. Because the particles are so small, shale often has a smooth feel.

**Sidewinding**
A way of moving used by some desert snakes. Sidewinders throw their bodies through the air, instead of slithering across the ground.

**Species**
A single kind of plant, animal, or other living thing.

**Spore**
A tiny speck that is like a seed, but much smaller and simpler. Ferns and fungi both spread by making spores.

**Spring**
A place where water in the ground flows out onto the surface. In some parts of the world, spring water is hot, because it is heated by volcanic rocks underground.

**Summit**
The top of a mountain.

**Vegetation**
All the plants that grow in a particular place.

**Vine**
Any plant that grows upward by twisting its way around a support.

**Volcanic hot spot**
A place where hot lava comes up from deep in the Earth's crust. Unlike ordinary volcanoes, hot spots can stay active for millions of years.

# Index

# Credits

David Burnie would like to thank Kim Dennis-Bryan, for her valuable help as consultant, Marilou Prokopiou and Smiljka Surla for design, and in particular Andrea Mills for editing and contributing to the text.

Dorling Kindersley would like to thank Lynn Bresler for the index and proofreading, Fran Vargo for picture research, and Paul Beebee and the team at Beehive Illustration.

The publisher would also like to thank the following for their kind permission to reproduce their photographs:

(Key: a–above; b–below/bottom; c–center; l–left; r–right; t–top)

6 Corbis: Roger Ressmeyer (cl); Galen Rowell (br); zefa/Werner H. Mueller (bl). 7 Photoshot: World Pictures/Rick Strange (cl). 8 Getty Images: The Image Bank/Kerrick James (b). 8–9 SuperStock: Carmel Studios. 9 Corbis: Craig Lovell (bl); Marc Muench (ca); Ron Watts (br). NOAA: Landsat (tr). SuperStock: Dan Leffel (cb). 12 FLPA: Minden Pictures/Frans Lanting (br). 13 Alamy Images: William Leaman. 14 Bryan and Cherry Alexander Photography: (cb). Corbis: Galen Rowell (ca). FLPA: Minden Pictures (b). Getty Images: National Geographic/Maria Stenzel (t). 14–15 Bryan and Cherry Alexander Photography. 15 Corbis: Rick Price (c). Science Photo Library: Doug Allan (b). 18 Bryan and Cherry Alexander Photography: (r). 19 naturepl.com: Doug Allan (tr). 20 Alamy Images: Jacques Jangoux (c); Sue Cunningham Photographic (b). 20–21 Altitude: Arthus-Bertrand Yann. 21 Alamy Images: Edward Parker (b); Sue Cunningham Photographic (ca) (cb). Corbis: Sygma/

Collart Herve (t). 26–27 Corbis: Bo Zaunders. 27 Alamy Images: blickwinkel (bl); David Robertson (cr). Corbis: Yann Arthus-Bertrand (tl); Sygma/Giry Daniel (br). Still Pictures: Thomas Haertrich (cl). SuperStock: Yoshio Tomii (tr). 31 Alamy Images: tbkmedia.de (br). 32 Corbis: Gabriela Staebler (cr). naturepl.com: Anup Shah (br). Photoshot / World Pictures: bild (bl). Science Photo Library: Bernhard Edmaier (cl). 32–33 Corbis: Nik Wheeler. 33 Alamy Images: Images of Africa Photobank (c). Getty Images: Stone/Christopher Arnesen (b). 36 Ardea: Tom & Pat Leeson (bl). 37 Alamy Images: Martin Harvey (c). Corbis: Joe McDonald (br). 38 Alamy Images: Bryan Lowry (bl). Photolibrary: Vince Cavataio (br). 38–39 Photolibrary: Joe Carini. 39 Alamy Images: Photo Resource Hawaii (cr). DK Images: (cl). Photolibrary: Joe Carini (tr). Science Photo Library: NASA (tl). 43 Alamy Images: Douglas Peebles Photography (br); Photo Source Hawaii/Jack Jeffrey (cl); Bill Waldman (t). Corbis: W. Wayne Lockwood (c). FLPA: Minden Pictures (clb); Mandal Ranjit (bl). Forest & Kim Starr: (crb). naturepl.com: Rod Williams (cra). Photoshot / NHPA: Stephen

Dalton (cla). 44 Corbis: Theo Allofs (cl). FLPA: Minden Pictures (r). Getty Images: Stone/Martin Barraud (l). Photolibrary: Doug Perrine (cr). 44–45 Imagestate: Hoa-Qui/Emmanuel Valentin. 45 Image Quest 3-D: Carlos Villoch (tr). PA Photos: AP/Ove Hoegh-Guldberg (tl). 50 Corbis: Peter Johnson (cr). Hemispheres Images: Franck Guizou (cl) (tr). naturepl.com: Ingo Arndt (tl). 50–51 Imagestate: Colin Mead. 51 Getty Images: Frans Lemmens (bl). Hemispheres Images: Patrick Frilet (br). 54 FLPA: Minden Pictures (r). 55 Alamy Images: Arco Images (c). 56–57 Alamy Images: Craig Lovell. 57 Alamy Images: mediacolor's (clb). Camera Press: Gamma/Aalain Buu (tr). Corbis: Galen Rowell (tl). NASA: (bl). naturepl.com: Leo & Mandy Dickinson (crb). Photolibrary: Colin Monteath (br). 61 Ardea: Tom & Pat Leeson (br). Photoshot / NHPA: Andy Rouse (t).

All other images © Dorling Kindersley
For further information see:
www.dkimages.com